Cobalt Blue Glass

Monica Lynn Clements
and
Patricia Rosser Clements

Schiffer Publishing Ltd®

4880 Lower Valley Road, Atglen, PA 19310 USA

Dedication

*We dedicate this book to
collectors of cobalt blue glass.*

Designed by Blair Loughrey
Typeset in Dutch 801 RmHd Bt/ZapfHumnst BT

ISBN: 0-7643-0685-5
Printed in China

Published by Schiffer Publishing Ltd.
4880 Lower Valley Road
Atglen, PA 19310
Phone: (610) 593-1777; Fax: (610) 593-2002
E-mail: Schifferbk@aol.com
Please write for a free catalog.
This book may be purchased from the publisher.
Please include $3.95 for shipping.

In Europe Schiffer books are distributed by
Bushwood Books
6 Marksbury Avenue
Kew Gardens
Surrey TW9 4JF England
Phone: 44 (0) 181 392-8585; Fax: 44 (0) 181 392-
9876
E-mail: Bushwd@aol.com

Please try your bookstore first.

We are interested in hearing from authors
with book ideas on related subjects.

Contents

Acknowledgments

We had the great pleasure of meeting many collectors with beautiful examples of cobalt blue glass. This book would not have been possible without their contributions. A special thanks to Ruby Henderson—for her time, enthusiasm, and hospitality! Also, thanks to Mary Moon for her wisdom.

Introduction

Cobalt blue glass takes many forms. Collectors choose from Depression Era glassware, elegant glassware, reproduction pieces, and a variety of collectible items. While the older glass is sought after, reproduction pieces and new cobalt blue glass items have fared well. Collectors most often consider the design rather than the age of an item, which has contributed to the enduring interest in collecting cobalt blue glass.

In the following pages, we offer a cross section of what is available to the collector. We showcase the wide ranging appeal of cobalt blue glass through the following examples. With the availability of this eye-catching blue glass, the only limit to the collector is how much he or she wishes to invest.

The purpose of this book is not to set firm prices but to serve as a guide. The prices reflect observations of the authors based on their experience in both buying and selling cobalt blue glass nationwide.

Chapter One
History

The ancient Egyptians manufactured colored glass from impurities found in raw materials. The Romans perfected this method. Cobalt blue glass can be traced back to ancient civilizations. In Mycenae, around 1400 B.C., the production of cobalt glass reached its peak. The glass was used in the making of jewelry and dishes. The stained glass windows of cathedrals throughout Europe evidence the popularity of this glass.

In ancient times, men discovered the value of cobalt, an ore similar in appearance to silver. During the glass making process, the addition of a small amount of this material turned glass the deep blue we now know as cobalt blue.

Examples of cobalt blue glass from the Depression Era exemplify the diversity of glass available to enthusiasts. Besides being known as cobalt blue, these companies sometimes referred to the color as Dark Blue, Deep Blue, or Ritz Blue. For example, the Macbeth-Evans Glass Company introduced the American Sweetheart pattern in the 1930s, which included pieces in Ritz Blue.

The Hazel Atlas Company produced the most well-known lines of cobalt blue glass with its Moderntone, Shirley Temple, and Royal Lace patterns. These three patterns will be forever linked. In her book, *Colored Glassware of the Depression Era*, Hazel Marie Weatherman recounts the dilemma the company faced after a precise number of Shirley Temple pieces had been made. With the vats of blue glass that remained at the factory, the company decided to use the extra glass to manufacture the Moderntone and Royal Lace patterns.

Moderntone in Deep Blue first appeared in 1934. The Hazel Atlas Glass Company offered this glassware until the 1950s. The simplicity of this pattern made it ideal for everyday use and ensured its popularity.

Pair of 4.75-inch tumblers from the Hazel Atlas Glass Company's Aurora pattern. *Courtesy of Mary Liles*. $75-85 each.

The Shirley Temple line consisted of cobalt blue glass with a white decal bearing the likeness of Shirley Temple. Although there is no record of how much was produced, the Hazel Atlas Glass Company made this glassware. Reproduction pieces of the Shirley Temple ware have appeared, and this new glassware has proved as popular with collectors as the original ware.

Hazel Atlas began production of Royal Lace in 1934, and production of this elegant looking line continued until 1941. Its intricate design makes it a popular choice for collectors today.

Above: **Left**. 4.5-inch reproduction Shirley Temple pitcher. $45-55.
Right. 4-inch reproduction Shirley Temple cup. $35-45. The Shirley Temple pitcher and cup are *Courtesy of Darlene Dixon.*

Left: **Left**. 4.25-inch Shirley Temple pitcher. $125-150.
Front and center back. Shirley Temple bowl, 6" in diameter. $95-125.
Right. Shirley Temple 4.25-inch pitcher. $125-150. The Shirley Temple pitchers and bowls are *Courtesy of Ruby Henderson.*

Left. 3-inch Moderntone creamer. $20-30.
Center. Moderntone butter dish with metal lid. $150-175.
Right. 3-inch Moderntone sugar. $25-35.
The Moderntone creamer, butter dish, and sugar are *Courtesy of Ruby Henderson*.

Left and **right**. Two 10 oz. tumblers from the Hazel Atlas Glass Company's Royal Lace pattern. $125-150 each.
Center. Two 12 oz. tumblers from the Hazel Atlas Glass Company's Royal Lace pattern. $95-125 each. The Royal Lace tumblers are *Courtesy of Mary Liles*.

Other companies introduced cobalt blue glass pieces into their Depression glass patterns. In the late 1920s, the Diamond Glassware Company offered cobalt blue pieces in the Victory pattern. Hazel Atlas introduced cobalt blue glass pieces in its Aurora line, New Century pattern, Florentine No. 1, Florentine No. 2, Hairpin, Ships and Sailboats, and Starlight. The Fenton Glass Company made available cobalt blue pieces to compliment its Lincoln Inn pattern. The Moondrops pattern and Radiance pattern by New Martinsville Glass Company provided cobalt blue pieces that are popular with collectors. Paden City Glass Company's cobalt blue glass pieces exist in the Orchid pattern and the Peacock & Wild Rose pattern. Westmoreland Glass Company showcased cobalt blue pieces in the English Hobnail Line. Collectors continue to discover long forgotten cobalt blue glass pieces from Depression Era patterns .

Along with Shirley Temple ware, other reproduction pieces of Depression glass patterns have appeared. Cameo, Cherry Blossom, Mayfair, and Sharon reproduction pieces in cobalt blue glass represent some of the choices available to collectors. Other reproduction items include copies of children's sets. Northwood glassware reproductions were also found. Despite their newness, these pieces remain quite popular as additions to collections.

Left. 3-inch reproduction of the Federal Glass Company's Sharon sugar bowl. $35-45.
Right. 3.25-inch reproduction of the Federal Glass Company's Sharon creamer. $25-35.

Left. 2.5-inch reproduction Cameo pattern cup with one handle. $15-25.
Center. 2.5-inch reproduction Cameo pattern cup with two handles. $20-30.
Right. Covered dish with cow. $20-30.
The items are *Courtesy of Karen Braswell*.

Reproduction covered dish of the Northwood grape pattern. *Courtesy of Karen Braswell.* $45-55.

7.5-inch reproduction of Northwood hat pin holder. *Courtesy of Darlene Dixon.* $45-55.

A long list of Depression Era companies designed elegant cobalt blue glassware. The pieces offered were not for everyday use but for more formal dining and entertaining. For example, the Morgantown Glass Company had a line of elegant glassware known as the Golf Ball pattern. The Cambridge Glass Company created glassware with overlay designs. An endless selection of elegant glassware awaits the collector interested in Depression Era cobalt blue glass.

Cambridge Glass Company covered dish with floral overlay design. $125-150.

11.5 inch in diameter bowl with sterling silver overlay. $95-125.

Left and **right**. Morgantown Glass Company candlesticks in Golf Ball pattern. $225-250.
Center. Morgantown Glass Company Golf Ball pattern open compote, 5.5" x 6". $225-250.

Left. 6.5-inch cut glass cruet with clear glass stopper. $55-65.
Right. 3.25-inch Cambridge Glass Company bottle with clear glass handle. $125-150.

Various companies have produced eye-catching decorative items made of cobalt blue glass. Such companies as the Fenton Glass Company have made baskets in cobalt blue. Fenton has continued the tradition of producing fine cobalt blue pieces with its line of eggs and slippers. Another company that produced distinctive looking slippers was the Degenhart Glass Company. Animals in every shape and size have remained available to the collector. For example, the Imperial Glass Company produced interesting varieties of animals in cobalt blue glass.

Fenton Glass Company basket. *Courtesy of Gayle Makowski*. $75-95.

10.75-inch Art glass basket. *Courtesy of Ruby Henderson*. $125-150.

9-inch ruffled basket. *Courtesy of Ruby Henderson*. $75-95.

7.25-inch Arkansas blown glass basket. *Courtesy of Karen Braswell*. $50-60.

Left. 9.25-inch basket with clear glass handle. $65-85.
Right. 7.25-inch Arkansas blown glass basket. $50-60.
The baskets are *Courtesy of Karen Braswell*.

Left. Hand-painted Fenton Glass Company egg on pedestal with floral motif. $50-60.
Right. Hand-painted Fenton Glass Company egg on pedestal with ship motif. $50-60.
The Fenton eggs are *Courtesy of Memory Lane Mall, Atlanta, Texas*.

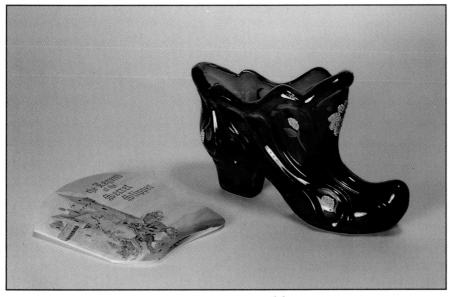

Fenton Glass Company 3-inch tall slipper. *Courtesy of Memory Lane Mall*. $50-60.

Left. Degenhart Glass Company 2-inch pitcher. $25-35.
Center. Degenhart heart box with lid, 3" x 3.25". $45-55.
Right. 2.25-inch tall Degenhart slipper. $45-55. The cobalt blue glass items are *Courtesy of Ruby Henderson*.

Left. Imperial Glass Company 6-inch horse. $55-75.
Center. Imperial Glass Company 3.75-inch rocking horse. $45-55.
Right. 4.5-inch rooster. $45-55. The horses and rooster are *Courtesy of Darlene Dixon*.

Avon Products, Inc. has offered an array of cobalt blue glass items to customers. The Fostoria Glass Company, long known for its quality designs, has produced glassware for Avon in the George and Martha Washington pattern. Among the numerous cobalt blue glass items produced by Avon, the company makes available such items as cruets, cologne bottles, and salt and pepper shakers.

Fostoria "Designed for Avon" 5.5-inch pitcher. *Courtesy of Mary Liles*. $65-75.

Above: Fourteen Fostoria "Designed for Avon" 8-inch glasses with George and Martha Washington. *Courtesy of Mary Liles.* $45-55 each.

Right: Fostoria "Designed for Avon" platter with likeness of Mount Vernon. *Courtesy of Mary Liles.* $95-125.

A popular area of collecting in cobalt blue glass is kitchenware. Although the nature of kitchenware has changed with reproduction pieces, refrigerator boxes, measuring cups, mixing bowls, rolling pins, and the like exist in cobalt blue glass. Items from Taiwan have taken on the look of Depression Era kitchenware. For example, a reproduction reamer, similar to those produced by the Hazel Atlas Glass Company, has become popular with collectors.

A type of cobalt glass not always considered with Depression glass or elegant glass is carnival glassware.

This type of glassware was first manufactured in the early 1900s, and its production continued into the 1920s. Although several companies produced this glassware in a variety of colors, the Fenton Glass Company and the Imperial Glass Company were only two of the companies to offer this iridescent glass in cobalt blue. In the early 1980s, the Imperial Glass Company reproduced selected iridescent pieces in cobalt blue glass.

10.5-inch Hazel Atlas Glass Company cobalt blue glass bowl with metal and tongs. *Courtesy of Ruby Henderson.* $55-65.

Westmoreland Glass Company style reproduction reamer. *Courtesy of Mary Gene Moon.* $15-25.

6.5-inch Imperial Glass Company iridescent bell in shape of woman. *Courtesy of Karen Braswell.* $40-50.

Another view of Imperial Glass Company iridescent bell to highlight cobalt blue glass interior.

Chapter Two
Cobalt Glass Jewelry

Unless otherwise noted, the cobalt glass jewelry is *Courtesy of Mary Liles*.

Cobalt glass necklace. $125-150.

Three strand cobalt glass 13-inch necklace. $150-175.

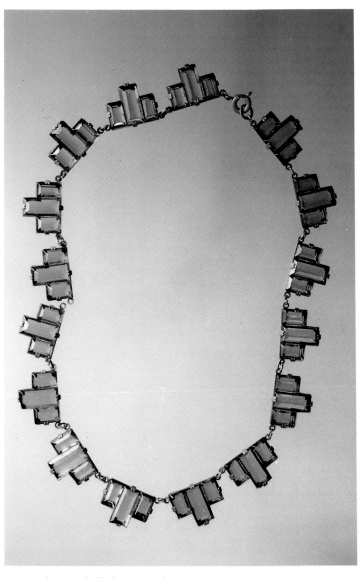

Trifari cobalt glass and silver metal
14-inch necklace. $150-175.

Art Moderne cobalt glass 16-inch
necklace. $175-195.

Gold metal and
cobalt glass dangle
earrings. $150-175.

Cobalt glass and
rhinestone brooch,
2.5" x 2.5". $75-95.

Left. Small cobalt glass with
rhinestones brooch with
floral motif. $75-95.
Right. Brooch with prong
set cobalt glass and
rhinestones. $65-85.

Left. Circular cobalt
glass brooch with prong
set cobalt glass in center.
$55-75.
Right. Cobalt glass
brooch with floral motif.
$75-95.

Left and **right**. Art cobalt glass earrings set with simulated pearls (some missing) and gold metal. $55-65.
Center. West Germany style pendant with cobalt glass and simulated pearls set in gold metal. $175-195.

Adjustable ring with prong set cobalt glass and gold metal setting. $45-55.

Left. Cobalt glass pendant. $55-65.
Right. Gold metal and cobalt glass bracelet. $75-95.

Gold metal necklace with simulated pearls and colored glass with cobalt blue glass pendant. *Courtesy of Arney Hayes*. $175-195.

Cobalt blue glass and gold metal earrings and necklace set. *Courtesy of Jerre Barkley*. $150-175.

Chapter Three
Cobalt Blue Cut Glass

10-inch cut glass vase with floral motif. *Courtesy of Pat Henry, Yesterday's Rose.* $125-150.

Above: Left. Large lead crystal vase. $60-70.
Right. Small lead crystal vase. $40-50.
The vases are *Courtesy of Diane Medellin*.

Right: 5.5-inch cut glass cruet with flower. *Courtesy of Diane Medellin*. $55-65.

10.5-inch cut glass pitcher with floral design. *Courtesy of Ruby Henderson*. $150-175.

Made in Poland 24% lead crystal 5-inch pitcher with floral motif. *Courtesy of Diane Medellin*. $95-125.

Box rose pattern cut glass 8.25-inch pitcher and six 3.75-inch glasses. *Courtesy of Ruby Henderson.* $225-250.

Above: Cut glass bowl with floral motif, 11.5" in diameter. *Courtesy of Ruby Henderson.* $95-125.

Left: 11.5-inch cut glass vase. *Courtesy of Ruby Henderson.* $125-150.

Pair of 8-inch lusters. *Courtesy of Ruby Henderson*. $225-250 for the pair.

8.25-inch basket. *Courtesy of Darlene Dixon*. $125-150.

11.5-inch decanter. *Courtesy of Ruby Henderson*. $150-175.

11-inch dish with lid. *Courtesy of Ruby Henderson*. $125-150.

Top left: 9.5-inch dish with lid. *Courtesy of Ruby Henderson.* $175-195.

Top right: Dish, 5.5" x 7". *Courtesy of Ruby Henderson.* $95-125.

Left: 14-inch vase. *Courtesy of Ruby Henderson.* $125-150.

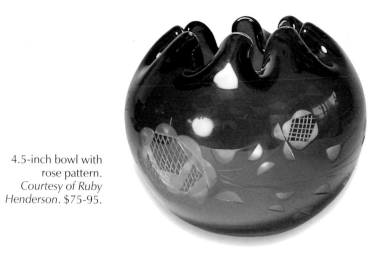

4.5-inch bowl with rose pattern. *Courtesy of Ruby Henderson.* $75-95.

4.5-inch paperweight. *Courtesy of Diane Medellin.* $50-60.

2.5-inch glass dish. *Courtesy of Darlene Dixon.* $95-125.

5-inch cut glass bowl, 8" in diameter. *Courtesy of Margaret McRaney.* $195-225.

Above: Made in Romania 10-inch cut glass pitcher with six 4.12-inch glasses. *Courtesy of Sarah Newton.* $225-250.

Left: 11.5-inch cut glass vase. *Courtesy of Karen Braswell.* $125-150.

Cut glass votive, 4" x 4". $40-50.

Chapter Four
Depression Era Companies

Right: Morgantown Glass Company Ritz Blue console bowl with alabaster trim from the Janice Old Bristol Line pattern, 9.25" in diameter. *Courtesy of Ruby Henderson.* $600-650.

Below: Duncan Miller Glass Company Caribbean pattern punchbowl and 12 cups. *Courtesy of Ruby Henderson.* $350-375.

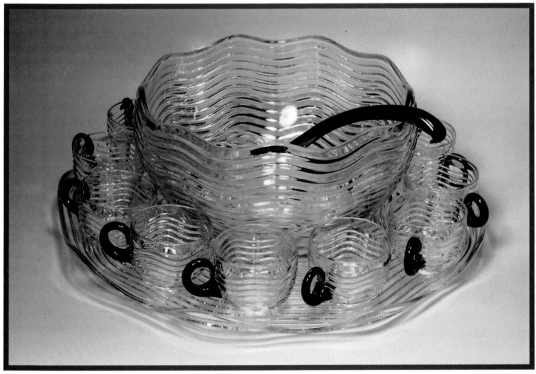

Front. Cambridge Glass Company Tally Ho punchbowl and 9 cups. Punchbowl is 5" x 10.5" and cups are 2.125" x 2.75". $225-250.
Back. Cambridge Glass Company sandwich plate, 18.75" in diameter. $75-95.

11.75-inch hand-painted basket in the Mary Gregory style. *Courtesy of Ruby Henderson*. $95-125.

Rear view of Mary Gregory style basket.

8-inch Mary Gregory
style night set.
*Courtesy of Karen
Braswell.* $75-95.

Imperial Glass
Company console
bowl, 8" in diameter.
*Courtesy of Ruby
Henderson.* $75-95.

Another view of
Imperial Glass
Company console
bowl.

Above: Imperial Glass Company relish tray, 6" tall and 8.5" in diameter. *Courtesy of Ruby Henderson.* $75-95.

Left: Cambridge Glass Company footed bowl with silver overlay, 11" in diameter. *Courtesy of Ruby Henderson.* $195-225.

Below: Another view of Cambridge Glass Company footed bowl.

Morgantown Glass Company tumbler with clear base. *Courtesy of Mary Gene Moon.* $35-45.

Left. Morgantown Glass Company Golf Ball water goblet, 6.75" x 3.25". $50-55. **Center left**. Morgantown Glass Company G olf Ball liqueur glass, 3.5" x 1.5". $50-55. **Center**. Morgantown Glass Company Golf Ball sherbet, 5" x 3.5". $35-40. **Center right**. Morgantown Glass Company Golf Ball liqueur glass, 3.5" x 1.5". $50-55. **Right**. Morgantown Glass Company Golf Ball wine glass, 4.75" x 2.12". $35-40.

Left. Heisey goblet. $250-275.
Right. Wine glass with clear stem, 5.5" x 2.5". $45-55.

Assortment of wine glasses with cobalt blue glass stems and bases, measurements range from 5.5" to 8". *Courtesy of Ruby Henderson.* $45-55 each.

Front left. 4-inch cordial glass. $45-55.
Front center. 3.25-inch cordial glass. $45-55.
Front right. 5-inch cordial glass. $35-45.
Back left. 4-inch cordial glass with clear base. $45-55.
Back right. 5-inch etched cordial glass with handle. $55-65. The cordial glasses are *Courtesy of Darlene Dixon.*

9.75-inch decanter and 2-inch glasses with silver overlay. *Courtesy of Ruby Henderson.* $195-225.

14.25-inch cobalt blue compote with clear stem. $55-65.

1920s 9-inch decanter with floral motif. *Courtesy of Ruby Henderson*. $275-295.

Left. 9.5-inch vase with silver overlay. $95-125. **Right**. 5.75-inch jar with lid. $75-95. The vase and dish are *Courtesy of Ruby Henderson*.

King's Crown 3-inch sherbet dish. *Courtesy of Mary Liles*. $20-30.

Left: **Front**. Two 4.5-inch King's Crown tumblers. $15-25 each.
Back. Three 6-inch King's Crown tumblers. $35-45 each.
The tumblers are *Courtesy of Mary Liles*.

Below: Lotus Glass Company bowl. $195-225.

Cambridge Glass Company console bowl, 10" in diameter. *Courtesy of Ruby Henderson*. $75-95.

Pair of L. E. Smith Glass Company 7.5-inch footed urn vases. *Courtesy of Ruby Henderson*. $125-150 for the pair.

Ruffled bowl, 11.5" in diameter. *Courtesy of Ruby Henderson*. $65-95.

Bowl with flower motif, 10" in diameter. *Courtesy of Ruby Henderson*. $85-95.

Westmoreland Glass Company 4.5-inch Hobnail finger bowl. *Courtesy of Ruby Henderson*. $45-55.

Bowl, 10.5" in diameter. $65-95.

Above: Duncan & Miller ruffled bowl, 10.5" in diameter. $75-95.

Left: Dish, 5.75" x 9.25". $75-95.

Below: Imperial Glass Company footed bowl, 10" in diameter. *Courtesy of Mary Liles*. $65-95.

Left. Vase, 4.75" x 4.25". $50-60.
Right. Vase, 6" x 3.75". $45-55.

Pair of vases, 4.25" x 4". $50-60 for the pair.

Sectioned relish tray, 8.5" x 8". *Courtesy of Ruby Henderson.* $55-65.

Top: Sectioned condiment dish on silver tray, 11" in diameter. *Courtesy of Ruby Henderson.* $75-95.

Above: Imperial Glass Company 14-inch platter. $35-45.

Left: Dish, 8" in diameter. *Courtesy of Ruby Henderson.* $45-55.

Above: Imperial Glass Company 18.75-inch platter. $55-65.

Left: Libbey Glass Company 9-inch plate. *Courtesy of Darlene Dixon*. $25-35.

Below: Tray with three inserts of clear triangles with incised fruit design, 10.25" in diameter. $55-75.

Sterling silver and cobalt blue glass sugar spooner with six 5.5-inch spoons, 8.5" x 6.125". $275-295.

Sectioned L. E. Smith Glass Company relish with handles, 15.25" x 6". $55-65.

13-inch candy dish with lid, quilting, and clear base. *Courtesy of Darlene Dixon*. $55-65.

5.5-inch compote with ruffled top. *Courtesy of Mary Liles*. $45-55.

Footed salt dish, 2.5" in diameter. *Courtesy of Darlene Dixon*. $15-25.

Left. Candleholder, 2.62" x 4.75". $15-25.
Right. Console, 10.5" x 2.75". $45-55.

Ice bucket from the Hazel Atlas Glass Company's
Sportsman's Series, 4.12" x 5.62". $45-55.

9.5-inch cocktail shaker with metal
lid from the Hazel Atlas Glass
Company's Ships Series. $45-55.

Three 10.5 oz. 4.75-inch water glasses from the
Hazel Atlas Glass Company's Sportsman's Series.
Courtesy of Memory Lane Mall. $25-35 each.

Above: Ash tray from the Hazel Atlas Glass Company's Ships Series. *Courtesy of Ruby Henderson.* $20-30.

Left: Cocktail shaker (without lid) from the Hazel Atlas Glass Company's Sportsman's Series. *Courtesy of Pat Henry, Yesterday's Rose.* $35-45.

Back left. Kraft Cheese dish with cover. $25-35.
Front center. 5.12-inch dish. $15-25.
Back right. Ruffled dish with clear handle, 5.5" x 1.75". $25-35.

Inside view of covered dish with lid. *Courtesy of Darlene Dixon.* $35-45.

Covered dish with another view of lid.

Depression Era 2.5-inch tall mayo dish, 4.5" in diameter. *Courtesy of Sarah Newton.* $25-35.

L. E. Smith Glass Company's Mt. Pleasant Pattern

Front. Two handled bowls, 6" in diameter. $35-45 each.
Back. Two handled 7-inch platter. $35-45.
The bowls and platter are *Courtesy of Ruby Henderson*.

Top. Two handled bowl, 6" in diameter. $35-45.
Bottom. Two handled 7-inch platter. $35-45.
The bowl and platter are *Courtesy of Ruby Henderson*.

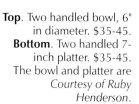

Left. 2.75-inch creamer. $30-40.
Right. 2.75-inch sugar. $30-40.
Mt. Pleasant cream and sugar are *Courtesy of Ruby Henderson*.

Left and **right**. Two 6.5-inch saucers. $25-35 each. **Center**. 8-inch plate. $30-40.

Two 4.75-inch L. E. Smith Glass Company candleholders. *Courtesy of Ruby Henderson.* $65-75 for the pair.

Three L. E. Smith Glass Company Two Handled Footed Bon-bon dishes, 6.5" in diameter. *Courtesy of Ruby Henderson.* $45-55 each.

Two handled cream soups. $35-45 each.

Hazel Atlas Glass Company's Moderntone Pattern

Above: **Left** and **right**. 2.5-inch covered condiment dish with spoon. $35-45 each.
Center. 3-inch covered mustard. $55-65.
The covered dishes are *Courtesy of Ruby Henderson.*

Right: **Left** and **right**. 4-inch glass. $50-60.
Center. 5-inch glass. $45-55.
The glasses are *Courtesy of Ruby Henderson.*

Front. 6-inch sherbet plate. $10-15.
Center left. 6.75-inch salad plate. $15-20.
Center right. 7.75-inch luncheon plate. $25-35.
Back left. 9-inch dinner plate. $35-45.
Back right. 10.25-inch sandwich plate. $55-65.
The Moderntone plates are *Courtesy of Ruby Henderson.*

Left. 12-inch platter. $65-75.
Right. 11-inch platter. $75-85. The platters are *Courtesy of Ruby Henderson.*

Above: **Front left**. Custard cup. $25-35.
Front right. Berry bowl. $30-40.
Back left. Cup and saucer. $45-55.
Back center. Cream soup and saucer. $35-45.
Back right. Sherbet and saucer. $30-60.
The Moderntone dishes are *Courtesy of Ruby Henderson.*

Right: **Front left** and **right**. Pair of cups and saucers. $45-55 for cup and saucer.
Back left. Dessert plate. $15-25.
Back right. Saucer. $10-15.

Left. Dessert plate. $15-25.
Right. Sherbet. $25-35.

Three 8.88-inch dinner plates. *Courtesy of John C. Sirmans, Memory Lane Mall*. $45-55 each.

Butter dish
with metal lid.
$150-175.

Left. Moderntone custard
cup. $25-35.
Right. Unidentified cup
with handle. $20-30.
The cups are *Courtesy of
of Memory Lane Mall*.

Berry bowl, 8.75" in
diameter. $60-70.

Hazel Atlas Glass Company's Royal Lace Pattern

The Royal Lace items are *Courtesy of Karen Braswell*.

Front left. Cup and saucer. $55-65.
Front center. Sherbet dish with metal base. $50-60.
Front right. Cream soup. $45-55.
Back left. 6-inch sherbet plate. $25-35.
Back center. 10-inch dinner plate. $55-65.
Back right. 8.5-inch lunch plate. $45-55.

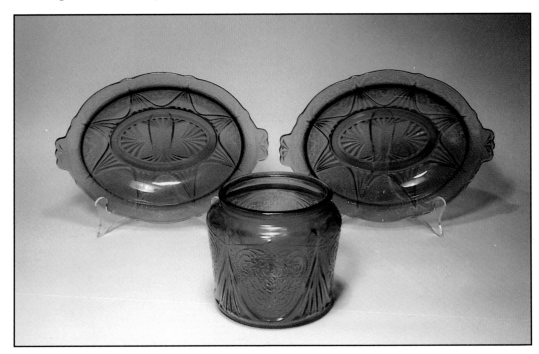

Left and **right**. Two 11-inch serving bowls. $65-75.
Center. Cookie jar without lid. $195-225.

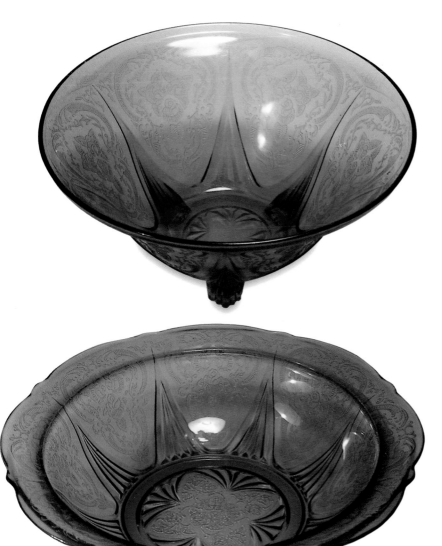

Top left: 5-inch footed bowl, 9.5"
in diameter. $75-85.

Above: 8-inch pitcher. $250-295.

Left: Serving bowl, 10" in diameter. $75-85.

Left. 5-inch
tumbler.
$150-175.
Center. 4.25-
inch tumbler.
$45-55.
Right. 3.5-inch
tumbler. $50-60.

8-inch pitcher with six 5-inch tumblers. $1200-1400.

Left and **right**. Two serving bowls, 10" in diameter. $75-85 each.
Center. 13-inch platter. $65-75.

Left. 4.25-inch creamer. $65-75.
Right. 4.25-inch sugar. $45-55.

Depression Era Pitchers and Glasses

***Above:* Left**. Hazel Atlas Glass Company 1938 40 oz. blown water pitcher. $30-40.
Right. Hazel Atlas Glass Company 1938 80 oz. blown water pitcher. $40-55.
The pitchers are *Courtesy of Ruby Henderson*.

Right: 1930s Hazel Atlas 54 oz. Ritz Blue glass pitcher. *Courtesy of Ruby Henderson.* $40-55.

Mayfair reproduction 6-inch pitcher and four glasses. $55-65.

Ringed pitcher and four glasses. $75-85.

Four 7.25-inch Imperial Glass Company tumblers. $10-15 each.

Reproduction children's set with 2-inch creamer, 2-inch sugar, and 2.75-inch covered dish. *Courtesy of Mary Gene Moon.* $45-55.

Reproduction set with 4-inch covered dish, 2.5-inch creamer, 2.5-inch sugar, and 5-inch covered dish. *Courtesy of Ruby Henderson.* $50-60.

Pieces from Akro Agate children's set.
Front. Three saucers. $8-10 each.
Center left. Creamer. $25-35.
Center right. Pitcher. $25-35.
Back. Four plates. $15-17 each.
The items are *Courtesy of Ruby Henderson.*

Chapter Five
Kitchenware

Hazel Atlas Glass Company cobalt blue glass bowl with metal and metal tongs. *Courtesy of Ruby Henderson.* $50-60.

Left back. 8.25-inch mixing bowl. $50-60. **Center**. 7.25-inch mixing bowl. $40-50. **Right back**. 6-inch mixing bowl. $30-40. The mixing bowls are *Courtesy of Ruby Henderson.*

Baker's Choice 17-inch rolling pin. *Courtesy of Diane Medellin.* $25-35.

Two 4.5-inch pitchers. *Courtesy of Mary Liles.* $45-55 each.

Reproduction Barnes 2.5-inch two piece reamer. *Courtesy of Diane Medellin.* $25-35.

Hazel Atlas style reproduction two piece reamer. *Courtesy of Darlene Dixon*. $20-30.

Reproduction reamer. $15-25.

Three 4-inch Crisscross refrigerator boxes (one without lid). *Courtesy of Karen Braswell*. $35-45 for box with lid.

Chapter Six
Condiment Pieces

Above left: 3.5-inch bowl in pewter holder. *Courtesy of Ruby Henderson.* $55-65.

Above right: 6-inch Cambridge candy dish. *Courtesy of Ruby Henderson.* $65-85.

Right: **Left**. 3-inch condiment dish with metal liner. $35-45.
Center. Condiment dishes. $55-65.
Right. Metal basket with cobalt blue glass. $40-50.
The condiment pieces are *Courtesy of Ruby Henderson.*

Three piece condiment set. *Courtesy of Ruby Henderson.* $95-125.

Left. 3-inch mayonnaise/sugar dish. $45-55.
Center. Two sugars with lids. $95-125 each.
Right. Sugar with lid and spoon. $150-175.
The condiment pieces are *Courtesy of Ruby Henderson.*

4.25-inch Occupied Japan salt and pepper. *Courtesy of Ruby Henderson.* $45-55.

Silver metal and cobalt blue glass sugar and creamer on tray. *Courtesy of Ruby Henderson.* $75-95.

Left. 8-inch sectioned condiment basket. $55-65.
Center. Divided condiment tray, 8" in diameter. $65-75.
Right. 6-inch rectangular sectioned condiment tray. $45-55.
The trays are *Courtesy of Ruby Henderson*.

Left and **right**. 2.5-inch silver salt and pepper with cobalt blue glass liners. $195-225.
Center front. 1.25-inch silver salt with cobalt blue glass liner. $95-125.
Center back. 3.5-inch Made in Japan metal salt and pepper with cobalt blue glass liners. $35-45.
The items are *Courtesy of Ruby Henderson*.

Above: **Front**. Eales two silver salts with cobalt glass liners and silver spoons. **Back**. Silver salt and pepper with cobalt glass liners. 125-150 for the set. The salts and salt and pepper are *Courtesy of Ruby Henderson*.

Right: Another view of Eales set in presentation box.

Left. Metal sugar bowl with lid and cobalt glass liner. $25-35. **Center**. Cobalt blue glass salad tongs. $50-60 for the pair. **Right**. Salt and pepper. $30-40. The items are *Courtesy of Karen Braswell*.

Above: **Back left**. Cobalt blue glass salt with sterling silver base. $150-175.

Back center. Sterling silver salt with cobalt blue glass liner and sterling silver spoon. $195-225.

Back right. Sterling silver salt with cobalt blue glass liner. $275-295.

Center left. Sterling silver salt with handle and lid with cobalt blue glass liner and cobalt blue glass spoon. $195-225.

Center right. Cobalt blue glass salt with footed sterling silver base and sterling silver spoon. $150-175.

Front. Small sterling silver salt with cobalt blue glass lining and cobalt blue glass spoon. $75-95.

The salts are *Courtesy of Ruby Henderson*.

Left: Six 1.33-inch salts (without lids). $15-25 each.

Below: Salt and pepper set on metal tray. *Courtesy of Arney Hayes.* $25-35.

Front. 2.25-inch salt and pepper. $45-55.
Back left and **right**. 3.25-inch salt and pepper. $40-50.
Back center. 4.25-inch pepper. $15-25.
The items are *Courtesy of Ruby Henderson*.

Left. 4.5-inch salt and pepper from Hazel Atlas Glass Company's Moderntone pattern. $50-60.
Right. 3.25-inch metal salt and pepper (without lid) with cobalt blue glass liners. $20-30.

Left and **right**. 3.5-inch salt and pepper. $15-25.
Center. Fostoria for Avon 5.25-inch salt and pepper. $35-45.

Above: Pressed dish with bird and cherries. *Courtesy of Mary Liles.* $55-65.

Left: 6-inch cruet. *Courtesy of Ruby Henderson.* $25-35.

Above: **Left**. Bowl, 5" in diameter. $15-25.
Top center. Love's Request pickle dish, 8" x 5". $35-45.
Bottom center. Ruffled bowl, 4.5" in diameter. $45-55.
Right. Fish, 6' x 6.25". $25-35. The bowls are *Courtesy of Ruby Henderson.*

Right: Footed salt cellar. *Courtesy of Ruth Derbin.* $25-35.

Chapter Seven

Decanters, Pitchers, and Glasses

Above left: 6-inch 1938 Hazel
Atlas 40 oz. blown water pitcher
with clear glass handle. $55-65.

Above right: 5-inch pitcher with
clear glass handle. $55-65.

Left: 9-inch clear glass pitcher with
cobalt blue glass handle and cobalt
blue accents. *Courtesy of Diane
Medellin*. $55-65.

Cambridge Tally Ho pattern 9-inch pitcher with six 3-inch juice glasses. *Courtesy of Ruby Henderson.* $195-225 for the set.

13.5-inch pitcher and six 5.75-inch glasses. *Courtesy of Margie Manning.* $275-295.

Made in Mexico 9-inch pitcher with two 7-inch tumblers (from set of eight). *Courtesy of Mary Liles.* $125-150 for the complete set.

11.75-inch pitcher with four fluted
9.75-inch glasses. $225-250.

Ring of Rings 10-inch decanter and six 3-inch
glasses. *Courtesy of Ruby Henderson*. $90-125.

10-inch cut glass night set with decanter
and glass. *Courtesy of Mary Liles*. $95-125.

Left and **right**. 5-inch silver metal and cobalt blue glass goblets. $45-55.
Center. 3-inch silver metal lid. $20-30.

10.25-inch decanter with clear stopper and clear base. $75-95.

7-inch brass decanter with cobalt blue glass liner. *Courtesy of Ruby Henderson*. $75-95.

Left. 7.75-inch decanter with clear pressed glass stopper. $65-75.
Right. 9-inch ringed decanter with pressed glass lid. $55-65. The decanters are *Courtesy of Ruby Henderson*.

Above: Made in Taiwan 9-inch decanter. *Courtesy of Mary Gene Moon.* $45-55.

Right: **Front left**. 24-inch swirl decanter. $45-55.
Front right. 19-inch decanter. $35-45.
Back left. Made in Italy 24-inch decanter. $45-55.
Back center. 24-inch decanter. $45-55.
Back right. Made in Italy 24-inch decanter. $45-55.
The decanters are *Courtesy of Darlene Dixon.*

Above left: **Left**. 9.25-inch decanter. $45-55.
Right. 11-inch American Legion 50th Anniversary 1919-1969 decanter. $50-60.
The decanters are *Courtesy of Darlene Dixon*.

Above right: **Left**. 10.75-inch decanter with gold ring design. $55-65.
Right. 10.25-inch decanter with clear stopper. $65-75.
The decanters are *Courtesy of Darlene Dixon*.

Right: **Left**. 12-inch jug. $35-45.
Right. Made in Mexico 8.5-inch pitcher. $30-40.

A trio of 9-inch Avon decanters. *Courtesy of Mary Liles.* $25-35 each.

1919-1969 50th Anniversary American Legion decanter. *Courtesy of Margaret McRaney.* $50-60.

Side view of American Legion decanter.

Back view of American Legion decanter.

Four 2-inch snuff glasses. *Courtesy of Mary Liles.* $15-25 each.

Trio of 9-inch clear champagne flutes with cobalt blue glass stems. *Courtesy of Memory Lane Mall.* $20-30 each.

Five 9.5-inch goblets (from set of eight). *Courtesy of Mary Liles.* $35-45 each.

Four 7.5-inch goblets. *Courtesy of Gold Leaf Antique Mall*. $10-15 each.

Four gold trimmed L. E. Smith Glass Company 6-inch footed tumblers. $18-22 each.

Four 4-inch blown tumblers. *Courtesy of Memory Lane Mall.* $15-25 each.

Left. 3.75-inch blown tumbler. $10-15.
Center. 3.5-inch blown tumbler. $10-15.
Right. 3.5-inch blown tumbler. $10-15.
The tumblers are *Courtesy of Memory Lane Mall*.

7-inch blown tumbler (with crack at base). *Courtesy of Mary Liles*. $15-25 as is.

Six Occupied Japan 4.25-inch cobalt blue glass and metal wine glasses on metal tray. *Courtesy of Ruby Henderson*. $75-95.

Set of five 2-inch glasses with silver metal holders on silver metal tray. *Courtesy of Ruby Henderson*. $65-85.

Trio of 5.5-inch cobalt blue glass mugs in the Art Deco style with silver metal holders. *Courtesy of Ruby Henderson.* $90-100 for the set.

Front left. 2.25-inch glass. $5-7.
Front center and **right**. Three 2.25-inch whiskey glasses. $10-15 each.
Back left. Heisey 3.25-inch cordial glass with clear glass stem. $55-75.
Back center. Three 2.25-inch whiskey glasses. $10-15 each.
Back right. 2.75-inch egg cup with silver metal holder. $35-45.
The glasses and egg cup are *Courtesy of Ruby Henderson.*

Set of six 3.5-inch highball glasses and an assortment of swizzle sticks. *Courtesy of Ruby Henderson.* $60-90 for the set. $15-25 for each swizzle stick.

Left. 6.25-inch goblet. $25-35.
Center left. Libbey Glass Company 7-inch goblet. $15-20.
Center right. 6.5-inch goblet. $15-20.
Right. 5-inch tumbler. $10-15.
The goblets and tumbler are *Courtesy of Darlene Dixon*.

Set of four 4.5-inch glasses. *Courtesy of Ruby Henderson*. $125-150 for the set.

Set of four Imperial Glass Company 4-inch glasses. *Courtesy of Ruby Henderson*. $90-125 for the set.

Chapter Eight

Candlesticks

Clear candlestick with cobalt base and gold decoration. $35-45.

Above: *7.5-inch candlestick. Courtesy of Mary Liles.* $45-55.

Left: *Pair of 9-inch candlesticks. Courtesy of Darlene Dixon.* $95-125.

Pair of 10-inch candlesticks that can be inverted to use as candy or nut dishes. *Courtesy of Ruby Henderson.* $125-150.

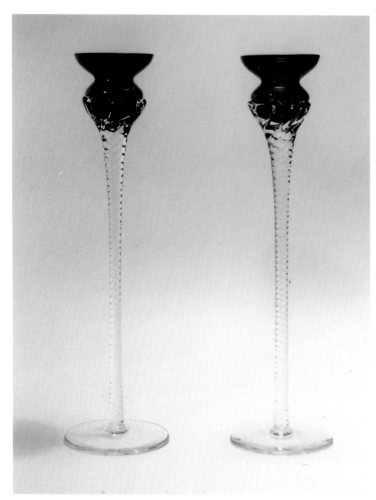

Above: 7-inch candleholder with metal handle. *Courtesy of Ruby* Henderson. $45-55.

Left: Pair of clear 12-inch candlesticks with cobalt blue glass at top. *Courtesy of Ruby Henderson.* $65-75.

Top: Pair of 8.5-inch candlesticks with angel motif. *Courtesy of Diane Medellin*. $55-75.

Bottom: **Left** and **right**. Pair of 6-inch candlesticks with angel motif. $55-65. **Center**. Seated angel figurine. $45-55. The items are *Courtesy of Diane Medellin*.

Above: Pair of 7.75-inch candleholders with silver metal base. *Courtesy of Ruby Henderson.* $45-55.

Right: Pair of 11-inch candlesticks in the shape of the Eiffel Tower. *Courtesy of Barbara Kay Smith.* $55-65.

Left. Pair of 2-inch candlesticks. $35-45.
Center. Votive with angel on three sides. $30-40.
Right. 2-inch candlesticks. $35-45.

Chapter Nine
Vases

Victorian Era two-handled
5.5-inch vase. $195-225.

Left and **right**. Pair of footed bud vases. $55-65 for the pair.
Center left. Vase with hand-painted floral design. $35-45.
Center. 9.5-inch bud vase. $20-30.
Center right. Ruffled vase with handle. $20-30.

Above: 3.25-inch vase with gold design in Southwestern motif. $75-95.

Right: 8-inch etched vase with clear base. *Courtesy of Diane Medellin.* $45-55.

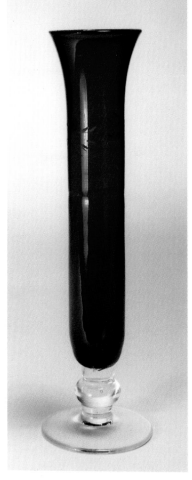

Pair of 6-inch vases with hand-painted floral design. *Courtesy of Ruby Henderson.* $65-85.

Above:
Left. 8.5-inch ringed vase. $25-35.
Right. 7.75-inch vase. $20-30.
The vases are *Courtesy of Ruby Henderson.*

Left:
Back left. 6.25-inch ringed vase. $25-35.
Back center. 7-inch vase. $30-40.
Back right. 6.5-inch vase. $15-25.
Center left. 6-inch ringed vase. $15-25.
Center right. 5-inch vase. $20-30.
Front. 4.5-inch vase. $15-25.
The vases are *Courtesy of Darlene Dixon.*

Left. 8.25-inch vase. $45-65.
Right. 8.25-inch ruffled vase. $35-55.
The vases are *Courtesy of Ruby Henderson*.

Left. 4.5-inch ruffled vase. $25-35.
Center. 5-inch vase. $20-30.
Right. 4.5-inch vase. $15-25.
The vases are *Courtesy of Ruby Henderson*.

Left and **right**. Two 7.25-inch vases with bubble decoration. $60-80 for the pair.
Center. Pair of 4.25-inch vases. $40-60 for the pair.
The vases are *Courtesy of Ruby Henderson*.

Left. 5.75-inch banded vase with ruffled top. $45-55.
Center. 3.5-inch banded vase. $15-25.
Right. 6.5-inch banded vase. $20-30.
The vases are *Courtesy of Ruby Henderson*.

Front left and **right**. Pair of 3.25-inch etched vases with floral motif. $55-65 for the pair.
Left. 8-inch bud vase. $35-45.
Center left. 8-inch etched bud vase with clear base. $45-55.
Center. 8-inch vase. $35-45.
Front center. 3.5-inch vase. $15-25.
Center. 8-inch blown vase. $35-45.
Center right. 7.75-inch blown vase. $35-45.
Right. 8-inch vase. $35-45.
The vases are *Courtesy of Ruby Henderson*.

Left. Pair of 8-inch bud vases. $65-85 for the pair.
Center. 5.75-inch vase with ring and ruffled edge. $35-45.
Right. Pair of ruffled 7.25-inch vases. $75-85 for the pair.
The vases are *Courtesy of Ruby Henderson*.

Front left and **right**.
Pair of 6-inch vases.
$55-65 for the pair.
Back left and **right**.
9-inch ruffled vases.
$45-55 for the pair.
The vases are
*Courtesy of Ruby
Henderson*.

7.25-inch vase. $65-95.

Left. 5.75-inch banded vase. $15-25.
Center. 7-inch banded vase. $25-35.
Right. 4.5-inch banded vase. $15-25.
The vases are *Courtesy of Ruby Henderson*.

Left. Westmoreland Glass Company 7.5-inch vase. $55-65.
Center. Vase with leaf motif. $50-60.
Right. 8.5-inch footed Finial Dolphin vase. $65-75.

8-inch vase in metal stand. *Courtesy of Ruby Henderson*. $45-55.

Two vases on metal wall hanging with ivy. *Courtesy of Ruby Henderson*. $40-50.

Three vases on metal wall hanging. *Courtesy of Ruby Henderson.* $55-65.

Two small vases on metal treble clef wall hangings. *Courtesy of Ruby Henderson.* $35-45 each.

Left. 5.25-inch ringed and ruffled vase. $45-55.
Center left. 4-inch vase with gold design. $45-55.
Center right. 3.25-inch vase. $15-25.
Right. 4.5-inch ruffled vase. $25-35.
The vases are *Courtesy of Memory Lane Mall.*

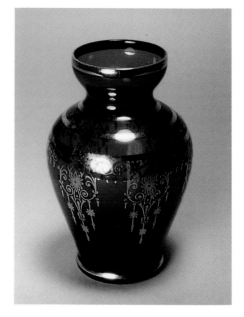

Top: **Front left**. 3-inch vase. $15-25.
Front right. 4-inch ruffled vase. $25-35.
Back left and **right**. Pair of 6.5-inch vases.
$65-85.
Back center. Blown 9-inch vase. $45-55.
The vases are *Courtesy of Darlene Dixon.*

Above: Venetian glass vase with gold
overlay. $45-55.

Left: **Left**. Blown 10-inch vase. $45-55.
Center. 8.5-inch vase. $35-45.
Right. Blown 17-inch vase. $45-55.
The vases are *Courtesy of Darlene Dixon.*

Left. Footed blown 8.5-inch vase. $45-55.
Right. 7.5-inch art glass vase with floral motif. $75-85.
The vases are *Courtesy of Darlene Dixon.*

Left. Arkansas blown glass 8.5-inch vase. $45-55.
Center. Arkansas blown glass 9-inch vase. $50-60.
Right. Arkansas blown glass 8.75-inch vase. $45-55.
The vases are *Courtesy of Darlene Dixon.*

Front left. 8.5-inch vase. $35-45.
Back left. 8-inch vase. $35-45.
Front center. 8.25-inch gold trimmed vase with hand-painted floral motif. $55-65.
Back right. 8-inch vase. $45-55.
Front right. 8.5-inch vase. $35-45.
The vases are *Courtesy of Darlene Dixon.*

Made in Italy lead crystal 9.25-inch vase. *Courtesy of Mary Liles.* $75-95.

Pair of 6-inch vases. *Courtesy of Mary Liles.* $65-85 for the pair.

Back left. 8-inch bud vase with clear base. $25-35.
Back center. 8-inch vase with clear base. $25-35.
Back right. 8-inch vase with clear base. $25-35.
Front left and **right**. Pair of 8-inch etched vases. $55-65 for the pair.
The vases are *Courtesy of Darlene Dixon.*

Left. 5-inch vase. $15-25.
Center. 10.5-inch bud vase. $35-45.
Right. 7-inch vase. $20-30. The vases are *Courtesy of Darlene Dixon.*

9-inch vase. *Courtesy of Darlene Dixon.* $60-70.

6.5-inch ruffled vase. *Courtesy of Darlene Dixon.* $75-85.

Top left: 12-inch ruffled vase with silver rings. *Courtesy of Darlene Dixon.* $75-95.

Above: 12-inch bud vase. *Courtesy of Memory Lane Mall.* $55-65.

Left: 10.75-inch vase. *Courtesy of Memory Lane Mall.* $65-75.

Left. 6.25-inch goblet. $25-35.
Right. 7.25-inch etched vase. $20-30. The glass and vase are *Courtesy of Memory Lane Mall*.

Left and **right**. Pair of 4-inch vases. $45-55 for the pair.
Center. 4-inch vase. $15-25. The vases are *Courtesy of Mary Liles*.

Left. 8-inch satin glass vase. $35-45.
Right. 4.66-inch tumbler. $10-15. The vase and tumbler are *Courtesy of Sybil Pugh*.

4.25-inch ruffled vase. *Courtesy of Mary Gene Moon*. $15-20.

8-inch block shaped vase. *Courtesy of Mary Liles*. $30-40.

Assortment of vases, ranging from 3.5" to 8.5". *Courtesy of Mary Liles*. Prices range from $15-55.

12-inch blue console ring. *Courtesy of Gold Leaf Antique Mall.* $85-125.

Pair of 6-inch tall hand vases. *Courtesy of Gold Leaf Antique Mall.* $65-75 for the pair.

8-inch Czech Art glass red vase with cobalt blue glass. *Courtesy of Gold Leaf Antique Mall.* $125-150.

8-inch footed and swirled vase. *Courtesy of Gold Leaf Antique Mall.* $55-75.

8-inch hand blown vase. *Courtesy of Karen Braswell.* $75-95.

Two satin glass vases. $35-45 each.
The vases are *Courtesy of Ruth Derbin*.

Unless otherwise noted, the lamps
are *Courtesy of Ruby Henderson.*

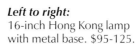

Left to right:
16-inch Hong Kong lamp
with metal base. $95-125.

21-inch converted Aladdin
lamp. $350-375.

32-inch hurricane lamp.
$275-295.

Pair of 9-inch lamps
with metal base.
*Courtesy of Mary Gene
Moon.* $80-95.

16-inch lamp with
handle. $90-125.

10.5-inch lamp with metal base.
Courtesy of Mary Liles. $195-225.

DIETZ FRIZALL N. Y. USA 6.5-inch lamp
shade. *Courtesy of Arney Hayes.* $55-75.

Left. 5.5-inch cut glass bell. $45-55.
Center. 7-inch "Joe St. Clair 1776-1976" bell. $25-35.
Right. Made in Czechoslovakia Bohemia crystal 7-inch bell. $55-65.
The bells are *Courtesy of Gold Leaf Antique Mall.*

Trio of 7.25-inch bell shaped Avon colognes. *Courtesy of Mary Liles*. $15-25 each.

Left. 6.5-inch Bicentennial bell. $25-35.
Center. 7.25-inch etched bell with butterfly motif. $35-45.
Right. 5.25-inch bell. $25-35.
The bells are *Courtesy of Darlene Dixon.*

Left. 7-inch ruffled bell. $45-55.
Right. 5.5-inch bell. $20-30.
The bells are *Courtesy of Darlene Dixon.*

Left. 6.5-inch bell. $25-35.
Center left. 6-inch Independence Bicentennial bell. $25-35.
Center right. 6.25-inch bell. $35-45.
Right. 5.5-inch cut glass bell with floral motif. $45-55.
The bells are *Courtesy of Ruby Henderson.*

Chapter Twelve
Perfume Bottles

Left. Perfume bottle with gold metal design and top. $20-30.
Center left. Perfume with clear glass and cobalt blue glass top. $25-35.
Center. Perfume. $35-45.
Center right. Perfume with floral top. $45-55.
Right. Geometrically shaped perfume. $45-55.

Left. Geometrically shaped perfume. $45-55.
Right. Perfume bottle with gold metal design and top. $20-30.

Left. Perfume bottle with floral top. $45-55.
Center. Large perfume bottle. $55-65.
Right. Perfume with clear glass and cobalt blue glass top. $25-35.

Left. Evening in Paris perfume. $45-55.
Center left. Perfume with gold metal design and top. $20-30.
Center. Avon perfume bottle with metal stopper. $25-35.
Center right. Victoria's Secret perfume bottle. $20-30.
Right. Perfume bottle in the shape of a mermaid. $45-55.
The perfume bottles are *Courtesy of Darlene Dixon*.

Above:
Left. Perfume. $55-65.
Center. Perfume with gold metal design and floral stopper with clear glass hummingbird. $45-55.
Right. Perfume with clear base and atomizer. $55-65.
The perfume bottles are *Courtesy of Darlene Dixon*.

Right:
Perfume bottle with applied design and stopper. *Courtesy of Mary Liles*. $75-95.

Left. The Angler Windjammer by Avon 4.5-inch cologne. $25-35.
Right. Artic King by Avon 4-inch cologne. $25-35.
The cologne bottles are *Courtesy of Memory Lane Mall*.

Left. Two Evening in Paris perfumes with tassels. $35-45 each. **Center**. Evening in Paris perfume. $45-55. **Right**. Evening in Paris perfume. $35-45. The perfumes are *Courtesy of Ruby Henderson*.

Trio of powder bottles. *Courtesy of Ruby Henderson*. $30-40 each.

Chapter Thirteen

Bottles and Jars

Left. 9.5-inch cruet. $25-35.
Center. 10-inch bottle with likeness of woman. $20-30.
Right. 8.5-inch bottle. $20-30.
The bottles are *Courtesy of Darlene Dixon*.

Assortment of bottles, ranging in size from
2.5" to 6". *Courtesy of Darlene Dixon.* $8-75.

Three medicine bottles. $15-65.

Left. Eyewash bottle. $45-55.
Center. Small glass with floral design. $12-14.
Right. Medicine bottle. $10-12.

Left. 1.75-inch jar with metal lid with floral design. $14-16. **Center**. 3-inch ink bottle with cork stopper. $18-20. **Right**. 1.75-inch jar with metal lid. $10-12. The jars are *Courtesy of Ruby Henderson*.

Three jars (without lids). $8-10 each.

Assortment of medicine bottles. $8-45.

Five medicine
bottles. $12-45
each.

Back left. Made in Italy Crownford China Co. jar. $55-65.
Back center. Made in Italy Crownford jar. $55-65.
Back right. Made in Italy "Aunt Mary's Pure Foods" jar. $55-65.
Front left. Made in Italy Granny's Products, Inc. jar. $25-35.
Front right. Made in Italy "The Sweet Shop" jar. $35-45.

Left. 9-inch 21 oz. bottle.
$55-65.
Right. 9.5-inch Made in
Taiwan 1 quart baby top
bottle. $18-20.
The bottles are *Courtesy of
Diane Medellin*.

Above:
Left. 6-inch eyewash bottle. $55-65.
Right. 6-inch medicine bottle. $12-18.
The bottles are *Courtesy of Mary Liles*.

Right:
14-inch barber's sterilizer with cobalt
blue glass cylinder that fits into clear
base. $95-125.

Above: Assortment of medicine bottles, ranging in size from 1.75" to 3.5". *Courtesy of Mary Liles.* $12-22.

Right:
Left. Medicine bottle. $10-12.
Right. Medicine bottle. $12-14.

Below: Assortment of eyewash cups, ranging in size from 1.5" to 2.75". *Courtesy of Ruby Henderson.* $45-85.

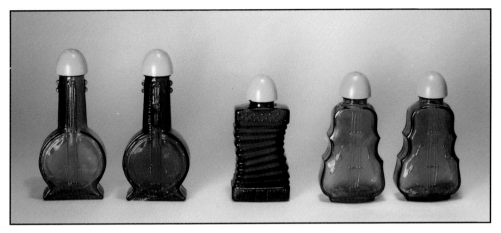

Left. 4.75-inch salt and pepper shakers. $45-55 a pair.
Center. 4.25-inch shaker. $55-65 a pair.
Right. 4.25-inch salt and pepper shakers. $45-55 a pair.
The salt and pepper shakers are *Courtesy of Ruby Henderson*.

Back left. 8.5-inch bottle. $18-22.
Back center. 3.88-inch jar. $15-18.
Back right. 2.5-inch jar. $15-18.
Front left. 5.25-inch bottle. $16-18.
Front right. 3-inch jar. $15-18.
The bottles and jars are *Courtesy of Arney Hayes*.

Left. 8-inch Bromo Seltzer, Emerson Drug Co. Baltimore Md. bottle. $25-35.
Right. 4.88-inch bottle with applicator for drops. $25-35.
These items are *Courtesy of Margaret McRaney*.

Chapter Fourteen

Animals

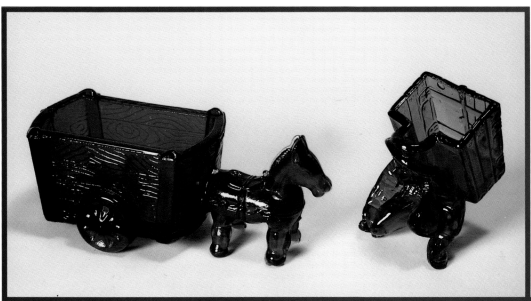

Left. 3-inch horse and wagon. $40-50.
Right. 4.25-inch vase with man. $45-55.
The items are *Courtesy of Darlene Dixon*.

Left. Altaglass from Canada 6-inch rabbit. $35-45.
Right. 5.25-inch dog. $35-45.
The items are *Courtesy of Darlene Dixon*.

Above:
Left and **right**. 2.8-inch covered hen. $35-45.
Center. 2.75-inch swan. $35-45. The covered hens and swan are *Courtesy of Darlene Dixon*.

Right:
8.5-inch hen on nest. *Courtesy of Gold Leaf Antique Mall*. $45-55.

Below:
8-inch hen on nest. *Courtesy of Darlene Dixon*. $55-65.

Above:
Back left. 3.5-inch duck. $45-55.
Back center. 3.25-inch dog. $45-55.
Back right. 4-inch collie. $45-55.
Front left. 2.5-inch seated deer. $35-45.
Front left center. 1.75-inch seal. $25-35.
Front right center. 4-inch standing deer.
$30-40.
Front right. 0.5-inch dolphin. $25-35.
The animals are *Courtesy of Darlene Dixon.*

Right:
Left. Horse. $35-45.
Right. Deer. $35-45.
The horse and deer are *Courtesy of Darlene Dixon.*

Left. Covered dish with rabbit. $45-55.
Right. Salt cellar. $15-25. The items are *Courtesy of Diane Medellin*.

Left. 3-inch mouse with clear glass ears. $35-45.
Right. 3-inch swan. $45-55. The mouse and swan are *Courtesy of Mary Liles*.

Cobalt and clear glass bird paperweight. $55-65.

Pair of 2.5-inch birds (right tail feather broken). *Courtesy of Darlene Dixon.* $35-45 as is.

Left. 4-inch lady figurine. $35-45.
Right. 5-inch bird. $50-60.
The items are *Courtesy of Darlene Dixon.*

Left. 4-inch blown glass swan. $45-55.
Center. 3.5-inch blown glass swan. $25-35.
Right. 4.25-inch blown glass swan. $50-60.
The swans are *Courtesy of Darlene Dixon.*

Left. 5.5-inch
blown glass swan.
$55-65.
Right. 6-inch
blown glass swan.
$55-65.
The swans are
*Courtesy of
Darlene Dixon*.

Left. 7-inch blown
glass swan napkin
holder. $45-55.
Right. 6.5-inch
blown glass swan.
$55-65.
The swans are
*Courtesy of
Darlene Dixon*.

Chapter Fifteen
Miscellaneous Items

General Electric clock, 5.25" x 5.25".
Courtesy of Darlene Dixon. $55-65.

Left. 2.5-inch inkwell. $15-25.
Right. Pair of 4-inch baskets. $45-55 for the pair.
The items are *Courtesy of Ruth Derbin*.

Assortment of cobalt blue
glass marbles. *Courtesy of
Darlene Dixon*. $2-15 each.

Left. 3-inch bird paperweight. $35-45.
Center. 3-inch egg paperweight. $30-40.
Right. 2.5-inch round paperweight. $35-45.
The paperweights are *Courtesy of Mary Liles*.

3.25-inch paperweight. *Courtesy of Karen Braswell*. $45-55.

Pair of slippers. *Courtesy of Ruth Derbin*. $25-35 each.

Left. 2-inch slipper. $25-35.
Center. 3.5-inch slipper. $35-45.
Right. 2.5-inch slipper. $30-40.
The slippers are *Courtesy of Darlene Dixon*.

Left. Cobalt blue glass hand. $55-65.
Right. 7.25-inch vase. $75-95.

Left. 5.5-inch bell with cobalt blue glass trim. $25-35.
Right. 7-inch reproduction hat pin holder. $45-55.

Top:
Tray for dressing table,
12" x 9".
$45-55.

Right:
Footed metal and
cobalt blue glass lighter.
Courtesy of Mary Liles.
$35-45.

Below:
4-inch long cobalt blue
glass train.
$65-75.

Left. 2.75-inch cup with bear design. $20-30.
Right. 3.75-inch Mr. Peanut cup. $25-35.
The cups are *Courtesy of Diane Medellin*.

Piggy bank, 4" x 3". *Courtesy of Gold Leaf Antique Mall*. $45-55.

4-inch "Remember the Maine" ship dish with lid. *Courtesy of Diane Medellin*. $45-55.

Gun, 4" x 7". *Courtesy of Diane Medellin*. $25-35.

Left. Glass box divided to hold two decks of Canasta cards, 4.5" x 6". $45-55. **Right**. 1.75-inch glass box. $35-45. The boxes are *Courtesy of Ruby Henderson*.

Pair of 1-inch ash trays, 3" in diameter. *Courtesy of Ruby Henderson*. $35-45 for the pair.

Back left. Flower frog. $15-25.
Back center. Metal box with cobalt blue glass lining. $20-30.
Back right. Box with lid and hand-painted design. $55-65.
Front. Square ash tray with gold trim. $25-35.
The items are *Courtesy of Ruby Henderson*.

Left. 2.5-inch footed toothpick holder. $45-55.
Center. 2.25-inch hat ash tray. $25-35.
Right. 2.5-inch blown pitcher. $35-45.
The items are *Courtesy of Mary Liles*.

Left. 2.5-inch toothpick holder. $35-45.
Center. Footed 2.5-inch toothpick holder. $45-55.
Right. 3-inch toothpick holder. $45-55.
The toothpick holders are *Courtesy of Mary Liles*.

Trio of 3.75-inch napkin holders. *Courtesy of Mary Liles*. $25-35 each.

Left. Candleholder. $25-35.
Right. Inkwell. $30-40.
The items are *Courtesy of Darlene Dixon.*

Left. Bottle without top.
$10-15.
Center left. Bottle. $10-15.
Center right. Avon perfume
bottle in shape of bell. $10-15.
Right. Lid. $5-10.
The items are *Courtesy of Darlene Dixon.*

Back left. Cup. $20-30.
Back center. Cup with handle
and bear design. $35-45.
Back right. Cup. $15-25.
Front left. Boot shaped salt or
pepper. $15-25.
Front right. Eyewash cup.
$35-45.
The items are *Courtesy of Darlene Dixon.*

Left. 3-inch square box with lid. $45-55.
Right. 2.75-inch Cambridge box with lid. $65-75.
The boxes are *Courtesy of Darlene Dixon*.

Above:
Left. Figure of woman reclining in dish. $55-65.
Center. Hand shaped dish. $20-30.
Right. Round dish. $15-25.
The items are *Courtesy of Darlene Dixon*.

Right:
Santa and sled. *Courtesy of Karen Braswell*. $35-45.

Left:
Mr. Peanut jar with lid.
Courtesy of Karen Braswell.
$55-65.

Below:
Four coasters. *Courtesy of
Karen Braswell.* $15-25 each.

Mexican plate, 18" in diameter. *Courtesy of Mary Liles*. $45-55.

Above:
Left and **right**. 7-inch blown swirl plate. $35-45.
Center. 10-inch blown swirl plate. $50-60.
The plates are *Courtesy of Mary Liles.*

Left: 11-inch platter. *Courtesy of Mary Liles.* $55-65.

Three new Libbey Glass Company bowls, 5" in diameter. *Courtesy of Memory Lane Mall*. $10-15 each.

Six 4.5-inch Libbey Glass Company mugs. *Courtesy of Kenneth L. Surratt, Jr.* $8-12 each.

Pair of ruffled bowls, 7.5" in diameter. *Courtesy of Mary Liles.* $15-25 each.

Above:
Left. 7.5-inch compote. $20-30.
Right. 5-inch jar with eagle design. $15-25. The compote and bottle are *Courtesy of Margie Manning.*

Left:
Bowl with silver stand, 2.74" tall and 4" in diameter. $35-45.

Chapter Sixteen
Iridescent Cobalt Blue Glass

Above:
Imperial Glass Company Cobalt
Lustre Rose 5-piece water set
with four 4.38-inch glasses and
8.75-inch pitcher. *Courtesy of Bill
Williams.* $175-195.

Left:
Left. 4-inch Imperial Glass
Company swan. $35-45.
Center. 6.5-inch Imperial Glass
Company goblet. $45-55.
Right. 2.25-inch Imperial Glass
Company hat. $45-55.
The items are *Courtesy of Mary
Gene Moon.*

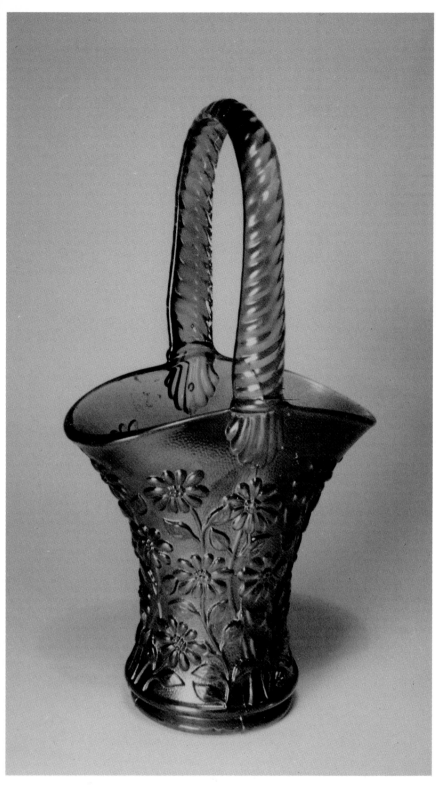

10.5-inch Imperial Glass
Company cobalt basket.
Courtesy of Mary Liles. $65-85.

Imperial Glass Company
cobalt mug. *Courtesy of
Kenneth L. Surratt, Jr.* $25-35.

Left:
Imperial Glass Company lustre footed bowl. *Courtesy of Mary Gene Moon*. $65-75.

Below, center:
Another view of Imperial Glass Company lustre bowl.

View of the bottom of Imperial Glass Company lustre bowl.

4.5-inch ruffled Fenton Glass Company cobalt iridescent vase. *Courtesy of Mary Liles.* $75-85.

Iridescent sugar and creamer on tray. *Courtesy of Mary Liles.* $75-95.

4-inch cobalt lustre bowl, 10.5" in diameter. *Courtesy of Mary Liles.* $20-30.

4.25-inch hand-painted cobalt blue carnival tumbler. *Courtesy of Jerre Barkley.* $65-75.

3-inch iridescent toothpick holder signed Joe St. Clair. *Courtesy of Margaret McRaney.* $55-65.

9.5-inch hand-painted cobalt blue carnival pitcher and seven 3.62-inch hand-painted cobalt blue carnival tumblers. *Courtesy of Virginia Giles.* $450-485.

Footed cobalt blue iridescent bowl,
12" in diameter. *Courtesy of Gold Leaf
Antique Mall*. $45-55.

View of the bottom of
footed carnival bowl.

Iridescent bowl with cobalt blue,
8.5" in diameter. *Courtesy of
Margaret McRaney.* $45-55.

Bibliography

Archer, Margaret and Douglas. *Imperial Glass*. Paducah, Kentucky: Collector Books, 1990.

Baker, Lillian. *100 Years of Collectible Jewelry*. Paducah, Kentucky: Collector Books, 1993.

Bredehoft, Neila. *The Collector's Encyclopedia of Heisey Glass 1925-1938*. Paducah, Kentucky: Collector Books, 1991.

Dayton, John. *The Discovery of Glass: Experiments in the Smelting of Rich, Dry Silver Ores, and the Reproduction of Bronze Age-type Cobalt Blue Glass as Slag*. Cambridge, Massachusetts: Harvard University Press, 1993.

Florence, Gene. *Collectible Glassware from the 40's, 50's, 60's . . ..* Paducah, Kentucky: Collector Books, 1994.

Florence, Gene. *The Collectors Encyclopedia of Depression Glass*. Paducah, Kentucky: Collector Books, 1994.

Florence, Gene. *Kitchen Glassware of the Depression Years*. Paducah, Kentucky: Collector Books, 1995.

Henzel, Sylvia S. *Collectible Costume Jewelry*. Greensboro, North Carolina: Wallace-Homestead Book Company, 1987.

Honey, W. B. *English Glass*. London, England: Bracken Books, 1987.

Jargstorf, Sibylle. *Glass in Jewelry: Hidden Artistry in Glass*. Atglen, Pennsylvania: Schiffer Publishing Ltd., 1998.

National Cambridge Collectors, Inc. *The Cambridge Glass Company 1930-1934*. Cambridge, Ohio: The Cambridge Glass Company, 1991.

National Cambridge Collectors, Inc. *Fine Handmade Table Glassware 1949 thru 1953*. Cambridge, Ohio: The Cambridge Glass Company, 1991.

Snyder, Jeffrey B. *Morgantown Glass: From Depression Glass Through the 1960s*. Atglen, Pennsylvania: Schiffer Publishing Ltd., 1998.

Weatherman, Hazel Marie. *Colored Glassware of the Depression Era*. Springfield, Missouri: Midwest Litho & Publishing Co., 1970.

Weatherman, Hazel Marie. *Colored Glassware of the Depression Era 2*. Ozark, Missouri: Weatherman Glassbooks, 1974.

Weatherman, Hazel Marie. *Fostoria: Its First Fifty Years*. Springfield, Missouri: The Weathermans, 1972.

Wilson, Charles West. *Westmoreland Glass*. Paducah, Kentucky: Collector Books, 1996.